Testimonials

"Scott's personal story is even more inspiring than his sales success and methodology. Finally, a leader that can break it down in the most challenging yet effective ways in this book. As a sales trainer, coach and speaker the past 18 years, I am eager to help make the sales word 'Process' one that deserves a capital 'P.' A MUST read for ANY sales professional!"

—Mike Lindstrom
Professional Speaker and Author of "*What's Your Story? Discover the Man Behind Your Dad*"
www.mikelindstrom.com

"If you are brand spanking new to sales or want to get into sales then this book will be your bible. Scott lays out his process for how to be successful in transactional selling in plain English. No theory just guidance."

—Trish Bertuzzi
Author of "*The Sales Development P*..."
CEO of T...

"Leese has managed to ac... pages, a complete playbo... ...ike the best at transactional s... ...om rep to VP. In this pithy treatise, Scott has boiled down his years of training and the essentials of how he's lead sales teams from failures to outsize successes into a short, digestible guidebook. Scott helped our company turn around our sales model and culture, and under his guidance, we embarked on a turnaround and growth path that led to over 200% in performance gains on a per rep basis in our inside sales team! His sage advice is now available to anyone wise enough to read this book, and the best part of it is that Scott's wisdom runs the gamut, so whether you're a rep just starting your journey, a sales manager looking to take his team to the next level, or a director or VP trying to push your organization even further, this book is for you!"

—**Matt Doka**
CRO at FiveStars

"There are over 13,000 books on 'sales' on Amazon. What makes this one different? The fact that Scott is a practitioner, not a theorist. He has had a long career as a technology sales leader (rather than just as a trainer or consultant), and an even longer one in the trenches. You can rest assured that everything Scott talks about in his book has been field-tested and refined by him personally hundreds of times."

—**Chris Orlob**
Senior Director, Product Marketing at Gong.io

Addicted to the Process

*How to Close Transactional Sales
with Confidence and Consistency*

SCOTT LEESE

Scott Leese Consulting, LLC

Addicted to the Process
Scott Leese
Scott Leese Consulting, LLC

Published by Scott Leese Consulting, LLC
Copyright © 2017 by Scott Leese
All rights reserved.

Scott Leese Consulting, LLC
PO Box 90954, Austin, TX 78709-0954
E-mail: addictedtotheprocess@gmail.com

Limit of Liability/Disclaimer of Warranty:

Publishing and editorial team:
Author Bridge Media, www.AuthorBridgeMedia.com
Project Manager and Editorial Director: Helen Chang
Editor: Katherine MacKenett
Publishing Manager: Laurie Aranda

Library of Congress Control Number: 2017901291
ISBN: 978-0-9984054-0-7 -- paperback
      978-0-9984054-1-4 -- ebook

Ordering Information:

Quantity sales. Special discounts are available on quantity purchases by corporations, associations, and others. For details, contact the publisher at the address above.

Printed in the United States of America

DEDICATION

To my children, Brayden and Caleb—who are already better salesmen than I am.

To my wife, Janet—for being the example of toughness I have always needed.

To my parents, Angela and Wallace—your support, discipline, and love have made me who I am.

To my grandmother, Nina—the strongest person I've ever met and will ever know.

To my brother, Taylor—the smartest kid I know, always one-upping me and pushing me on.

To my friends and loved ones—your encouragement, successes, and guidance made this book possible.

And to those who have struggled, suffered, endured, and overcome, I dedicate this book to you. You inspire the rest of us every day. My hope is that these pages motivate you to share your story as well.

CONTENTS

ACKNOWLEDGMENTS

As with most accomplishments, this book would not have happened without the support and encouragement of many people in my life. I would like to thank the following individuals who played a role in helping me develop this book by challenging me to hone my own Process. You remind me that we all have challenges and struggles; it's how we deal with them consistently that makes us who we are.

Thank you to Kay Kohen, a teacher who made a true impact on me as a person. You helped me develop an interest in psychology and showed me that understanding people is a way to understand yourself. Thank you also to all my coaches growing up (especially my Dad), who helped me better understand the true driver of success: overcoming obstacles, setbacks, and failures.

Thank you to all of my former teammates who encouraged me to train harder and more often, to step up and lead, and to celebrate my successes and learn from my setbacks: the members of my former soccer and tennis teams, my surf crew, my oldest and best friends, and former colleagues and collaborators. I'm lucky to say some of my best friends today are folks I have known nearly half my life or longer. You continue to push me to be better, even today.

I'm grateful to my family, friends, and mentors, including Taylor Leese, Mike Lindstrom, Richard Harris, Jonathan Dawe, and Lena Shaw. You were great sounding boards as I worked to make connections between sales, leadership, growth, and, finally, writing.

Thank you to my most loyal colleagues and business partners, including Scott Partlow, Claire Morris, Paige Drews, Daniel Molas, Matt Hernandez, and countless others without whom none of my successes would have happened.

To everyone who told me I couldn't or wouldn't do it, thank you for your part in encouraging me to share my story and to try to make a difference in the lives of some people who needed it.

I am grateful to those who stood by me and refused to let me quit, and who still refuse to let me give up even now. My mom, Angela Leese, for her unwavering love and faith in the healing process. My Dad, Wallace Leese, for having the wisdom and conviction to know when to push and when to encourage rest. To Garrett and Brian Gray, whose friendship saved my life during my illness. To Amber Eandi-Marinescu, for a lifetime of friendship and support. To Casey Gillispie and Taylor Smith, for struggling with me and helping me find a way to laugh and smile through it all.

Thank you to my wife, Janet, who plays the roles of wife, mother, therapist, doctor, and teacher in my life. Without your sacrifices, none of this would have ever been possible. To my sons, Brayden and Caleb: you inspire me to be better, and you make me proud every day.

Finally, thank you to Katherine MacKenett, Jenny Shipley, and the Author Bridge Media team for your editorial and publishing services. Your most valuable contribution was in helping me to bring structure and clarity to something I previously had been unable to nail down. I am grateful for your assistance in creating this book.

INTRODUCTION

Adrift

Sales is the garbage can of jobs.

When you don't know what to do with something anymore, you might choose to throw it away. When you don't know what kind of career you want or you've been "thrown away" by other choices, you might end up in sales.

Maybe you studied liberal arts in college, but nobody is hiring. Maybe you work in the retail or service industry, but you are tired of the hours or cleaning up spilled beer. You are ready for something more professional, but you are rudderless. You feel like a ship adrift in the ocean.

Maybe you've made some mistakes, and you feel there might not be a ton of options available. Life is just happening to you, rather than you deciding what you want and then setting a course.

You see the people around you doing more with their lives. Your friends are getting married, having families, and starting to make six figures. They're working more, and they're not as interested in going out on a Wednesday night to take tequila shots. Things are changing all around you, and you feel left behind.

You want to keep up. You think you're doing the best you can—but you want to do better. You need a way to get to the next level.

Why isn't it happening? you think. *Where's the sherpa to show me a better way up the mountain? What do I need to do?*

The Path to Success

There is a way to take your life back that leads to success, at work and at home. It all starts with making the decision to follow a proven path.

That path can be transactional sales. Transactional sales—as I refer to them in this book—have a short sales cycle, few decision makers, high volume, and a relatively low complexity of product.

The sales world may be where people end up when they have nowhere else to go, but you can decide to change your life through transactional sales. It can be a launching pad for the rest of your career.

And that launching pad leads to powerful change.

You will have a new sense of direction, and direction leads to self-confidence. As you have more success, your self-esteem will improve. You can replace bad habits with healthier ones, and then your productivity will increase as well. You'll be making smarter decisions outside of work, so you'll be prepared to perform at your optimal level inside of work.

No longer will you be working just to survive and pay bills. Instead, you'll be changing the direction of your life. Maybe now you can buy that new car you've dreamed about. Perhaps you want to take a trip to see more of the world. You might move into a nicer home, now that you can provide more for your family.

Transactional sales is a platform to success for the rest of your life. You hold the key to getting started in your hand—and in your mind.

If I Can Do It, So Can You

I'm living proof that the process in this book works. I was once that person who had lost control of his life.

I had no special talents or pedigree that gave

me any kind of advantage. My dad was a college professor and my mom was a nurse. They had no sales experience whatsoever. I played sports in high school and college. As an undergraduate, I studied psychology with a minor in religious studies, but I chose those only because they were interesting to me. At that time, I had no brain for business or making money.

I went to graduate school because I still didn't know what I wanted to do with myself. Then, right before I finished my master's degree, I got really, really sick. I was twenty-three years old.

I spent the next four years in and out of Enloe Medical Center, the Mayo Clinic, and the University of California, San Francisco (UCSF) Hospital, fighting for my life. At first, nobody knew why I was so sick. Then they discovered that I had an autoimmune disease—ulcerative colitis—which led to multiple abdominal surgeries.

I was fed every horrible drug you can think of to treat the disease and the pain: antibiotics, steroids, immunosuppressants, Dilaudid, Demerol, oxycodone, and even liquid morphine. None really worked.

I lost more than fifty pounds because I couldn't eat or drink. I couldn't walk or even stand up on my own. I was in constant pain. I wanted to die. Every waking moment was a struggle to survive.

During that period, I thought a lot about what I was going to do with myself once I got out of the hospital. I needed to make up for lost time. One of the first things I did when I was on the mend was to kick all the narcotics. Physically, I was a junkie. I got lucky and didn't have any mental or emotional addiction, so I went cold turkey. Everybody said it was a bad idea, but I figured, "I've already been through four years of hell—what's another week or two?"

When I recovered, it was the summer of 2004. I was twenty-seven years old, and I'd never really had a job, let alone a career. I had just gotten married, and I had no idea what I was going to do.

But I now had a family to support. So I made the strategic decision to go into sales. It was the only thing I could think of that would allow me to make as much money as possible, based on how well I performed and how hard I worked. It made sense to me as an athlete and competitor: you play well; you get paid well. You play poorly; you get cut.

In fact, I used a sports analogy when I went on my first interview. The cofounder of the company asked why I had no real work experience. I looked at the San Francisco 49ers pictures on the wall before replying, "I am going to be the best undrafted free agent that you'll ever find. All I need is a chance."

And it worked—he gave me that chance.

I got hired with twenty other people. We all showed up for the first day and went through training until it was time for lunch. Then they said, "Time to get on the phone."

Are you f***ing serious? I felt like I'd just been thrown to the wolves.

That first day was awful—rejection after rejection. I didn't even want to pick up the phone anymore. That night, I told my wife, "I'm not going back."

She paused. At the time, my wife was going to graduate school full time. I was our only source of income. "That's fine," she said neutrally. "You can quit. But then what?"

And it hit me like a ton of bricks: I had no plan B.

She was right. I had no choice but to dig in and figure it out. What the hell was wrong with me? Who quits so easily? That was not representative of the guy who had already fought major obstacles so hard for so long.

So I started going at it—*hard*. I came into work

around six in the morning and left twelve hours later. By that very first Friday, I was the last person from the group I'd been hired with who hadn't either quit or made a sale. I thought I was going to get fired at any moment, so I stayed late in the darkened office. Around nine thirty that Friday night, I was still cold-calling Hawaii, trying to take advantage of the time difference.

And that's when I closed my first deal.

It was like somebody flipped a switch inside me. It was the best feeling in the world, and I knew I wanted to feel it again and again. *I just figured it out!* The only reason I made the sale was that I was in the office, working on a Friday night, instead of going out with friends or making stupid decisions. I was alone at my desk, trying to make something happen, while most other twenty-seven-year-olds I knew were well on their way to needing a bottle of Advil the following morning.

That would be my path. If it worked once, I thought, it could definitely work again. I put in the extra effort, which allowed me to learn faster, and I kept doing it until I saw rewards.

If I can do it, so can you.

Every Day a Win

I'm lucky to be alive. I'm lucky to be where I am. And I'm lucky because after that first success, the deals just kept coming.

I had found a purpose: I wanted to be the best, and I wanted to help others do what I was doing.

I quickly became the number one salesperson in that company and was promoted to sales manager and then senior sales manager. I was named Employee of the Year and was also a finalist for Sales Manager of the Year.

Since then, I've been building, advising, and scaling inside-sales organizations for startups all across the country and even in Europe. I've carved out a niche for myself in this world. Founders come to me when they have a great idea and need to figure out how to sell it.

As of 2016, I've helped five different organizations grow. I'm particularly proud of the last two. Main Street Hub was ranked the seventy-third fastest-growing company in America in the 2014 Inc. 5000. The 2016 Inc. 5000 ranked OutboundEngine number ninety-five overall, number four in the state of Texas, and number one in Austin. In fact, OutboundEngine was voted one of the Best Places to Work in Austin for five years in a row. One of its offices was also on the Best Places to Work list for the greater Phoenix area.

The sales numbers that have developed in these places sound ludicrous, because the companies quickly go from no revenue to having a successful and repeatable sales process in just a few years. Hundreds, perhaps thousands, of people have gone through my training at these organizations.

Every day is a win when you're watching people grow and blossom. The beauty and the joy for me is knowing that I poured myself into providing people with new opportunities to hit bigger milestones—to do things they have never done before—and watching firsthand as they succeed. This experience has allowed me to continue to grow as well.

So I am telling you, if I can do this sh*t, so can you.

Light Your Fire

I want to show you how to hit the same milestones I hit myself—the ones I've successfully taught hundreds of transactional salespeople to hit. But for me to do that, you have to be open to what I have to say.

You have to be open to change. You have to be willing to do things you've never done before.

Take a moment now. Acknowledge that you don't know everything. Recognize that there might be a different way, a better way, to make some improvements.

It's important to read this book from start to finish, and to follow the Process. The Process is in place, in a specific order, for a reason. It's critical not to jump around trying to find shortcuts or to think that you have certain things already mastered. The path has been laid out for you. You simply have to choose to follow that path.

Once you're done reading, it will be time to apply what you've learned. This will affect every aspect of your life: the choices you make, how you work and how *hard* you work, how much you care, and how seriously you take it. It will affect you in ways you didn't think were possible, and perhaps in ways that terrify you.

A good friend I respect very much once told me that success boils down to one question: "How bad do you want to make it happen?"

This book should provide you with a shot of adrenaline that lasts long after you've closed it. Periodically, though, you're going to lose track of what has made you great. When that happens, come back to this Process, reference it, and remind yourself of how you became successful.

Use this book as the first step on your path to sales greatness. Light the fire within. Then return to rekindle it when you feel your flame burning low.

Now or Never

It's time to stop thinking about taking your life back and just do it.

The great thing about a career in sales is that you don't need a college degree. You certainly don't need an MBA from Harvard or Stanford. You don't have to be exceptionally gifted or acquire special skills that take forever to learn. What you do need is an intense desire to succeed and the willingness to hustle.

To get started, all you have to do is make a mental shift—and then make a commitment. Do what I discovered was a blessing in disguise: jump in without a backup plan. Go all in! You don't need to overanalyze it.

Then once you get started, you can use each opportunity as a stepping-stone to move forward from one place to the next. There is no perfect time to do anything, and there will always be an excuse not to start.

So what are you waiting for? This is your "now or never" moment. Let's choose "now."

Chapter 1

The Process

At the Plate

Imagine you're a baseball player going through a slump. You're not hitting home runs. It's been a while since you hit anything. You start to get obsessed with the struggle instead of focusing on success. You think, "I *need* to hit a home run!"

To try to turn it around, you tweak things—too many things. You change your batting stance. You start swinging at the first pitch every time. You chase every breaking ball. Do these frantic attempts to change ever work?

One of the first things they tell you in baseball is to stop worrying about the result and start focusing on the process. Stop focusing on hitting home runs, and get back to the basics. Get your batting stance situated: get on balance, keep your elbows up, bat back, knees bent. See the ball. See good pitches. Don't worry about how far or hard you are hitting it. Just try to make contact.

All of a sudden, you get a hit. You start to come out of the slump.

Once you are making contact consistently, you need to get to a place where you're driving the ball. You start to hit the ball hard, but in your next at bat, you hit a groundout. Then you hit a high, deep fly ball, and somebody catches it in the alley. But soon you hit a single. Then a double.

You hear your coach say to your teammate, "He's coming back." And before you know it, you're hitting home runs again.

You trusted in the process, you went back to the basics, you put in the time and effort, and it worked. This is how transactional sales will work for you too.

What Is the Process?

Before you can have faith in the Process of transactional sales, you have to understand it. So what is this Process, anyway?

The Process is the routine required to give you

the best chance for success in transactional sales. It is a methodology and series of habits, decisions, and actions. It's the way of going about every single sales call you make that gives you the greatest chance of being the best salesperson in the company.

Too many people in sales focus on selling what their product does. They constantly talk about features and benefits. But that's not how I think about things. I think prospects could not care less about your cool product and company, because they don't know they have a problem. Or if they do, they certainly don't think it's important enough to do something about it any time soon.

The Process I've come up with is mirrored after the addiction model.

With the addiction model, you first have to get people to admit they have a problem. Then you get them to understand why they should care about having this problem and why it's important to change. Then, and only then, can you get them into rehab. I think sales is very similar to this process.

With the Process, my first job is to get prospects to admit that they have a problem. Then they're ready for me to educate them on why they should care about having this problem. I have to communicate the need to solve the problem immediately. They have to see the value and feel the urgency of making this particular change. Only then are they going to be open to hearing about the answer to their problem. That's when I can talk about what the product does and present it as the solution, offering them the opportunity to take advantage of it.

If I just called you up to tell you about my company and what my product does, your first reaction would be, "What does this have to do with me?" Similarly, I can't just walk up to someone with a substance abuse problem and say, "I know this kick-ass rehab facility. You want to go?" The immediate reaction would also be, "What are you talking about? I don't have a problem." You can't solve people's problems until they acknowledge them and care about changing them—right now.

The Process is in place for a reason—to bring you the greatest chance for success.

Why Have a Process?

The Process provides a strategy to follow. It's a road map and a guide to help you get to where you want to go.

Generally speaking, when a group of new hires starts in sales, they're a bunch of inexperienced people running around trying to figure out what to do. If I let them just figure it out on their own, they're going to struggle, and they may never figure it out at all. I need to provide the right tools and the right guidance from the get-go. I need to reduce the time from inexperience to success.

The best tool for success is the Process. If you focus on it, rather than worrying about the outcome, the results will follow.

Too often salespeople are so fixated on thinking, "I need to close the deal," that their process breaks down. They get what I call "happy ears." They take shortcuts. If they're on the phone and the prospect shows any interest, they become overly excited and desperate. They jump ahead in the Process and skip over some parts. Their patience wears thin, and they get anxious to close instead of staying calm and patiently creating value and urgency.

When this happens, the odds of closing the deal are greatly diminished.

It's really important to stay dedicated and adhere to the Process all the time. When you believe in it, it works for you. If you follow the Process and pitch people the right way, it will work better than any other methodology.

And once you've learned this Process, it's important to keep using it. Don't tinker. When people first get started, they all make the same mistake: they follow the Process, have some success with it, and then think they have it figured out. They say, "Now I can put my own spin on it." And when they do, it falls to pieces.

The most common response I get from someone who started off strong but is in the midst of a sophomore slump is "I don't know what happened!" I ask, "What did you change?" And the answer is always "Nothing." Yet once we dive into the calls and the pitch and process used, it becomes painfully obvious that the person has strayed from what was working before.

I'm teaching you to do it this way because it works. And it will work consistently. If something is working, don't change it. Just get better at each of the steps within that Process.

Small Wins, Big Results

Getting better at each step of the Process can be explained using the Japanese business concept of *kaizen*.

Kaizen is the idea of making small, daily, continuous improvement. If you are struggling, you just need to pick one thing to work on and improve that small piece. Otherwise, it's easy to get overwhelmed by the big goals that you set for yourself.

For example, I used to have a goal to "read more." There was no way for me to feel any sense of progress toward that goal because it was too vague and overwhelming in its scope. It scared me off, and I actually read less because of it. But then I realized that the real goal was to acquire information about leadership, sales, and business. So I set the specific, smaller goal of reading one book per quarter. Reading one book in three months sounded attainable, so it motivated me to keep going.

Once I achieved my goal and was reading a book every quarter, I graduated to one book per month. It was a manageable goal that provided me with small wins, which reinforced my good decisions.

You want to be very specific with your goals. You need your goals to be measurable and achievable so you get wins under your belt that build up your confidence to keep going. There is a reason that powerhouse college football programs schedule games against Tiny No-Name University from the middle of nowhere early in the season—they are looking to get their rhythm and confidence going. Focusing on the Process will give you the small wins that eventually lead to the big results you want.

The World of Transactional Sales

People have been selling things since the dawn of humankind. Cavemen tried to convince other cavemen to search for food in a certain area. That method—one person attempting to convince somebody else of something—is sales.

There are more books about the sales industry than you could ever read in a single lifetime. One of the reasons I wanted to write this book is that I believe the world of transactional sales does not get the respect it is due. And I believe the beginning of one's journey into a sales career doesn't need to be so scary. Transactional sales—the specific world we're talking about in this book—doesn't get as much attention as the other areas of sales, and that's a shame.

For some reason, transactional sales has been seen as a less glamorous field than other forms of sales. It's not in the spotlight all the time. It can require a lot more grit and hustle, and some people find that grimier. Over the years, I have received feedback that demeaned the transactional sales world unfairly.

But there's no other world for me.

Working for a big corporate enterprise-level organization, where you work deals for years and wine and dine people multiple times to move prospects through a hundred different steps, sounds tedious and exhausting. (And you'll never convince me that it makes you a better salesperson!) If I were able to close only one deal a quarter, I'd get to go home only four days out of the year with that feeling of *I got a win today*. Where is the rush in that?

I'm too much of a competitor for that world. I want to go home every day feeling that I won or lost. If I won, I want to feel as if I'm on top of the world. If I lost, I want to feel like dirt, and I want to use that to motivate me to never feel that way again. And I want it all to start again tomorrow. I want to know each day I come into the office that I have the possibility of a kick-ass day. I need that hope.

There are a lot of new beginnings in transactional sales versus more traditional sales positions, where one relationship is nurtured over time. It's not that one is necessarily better than the other. It just depends on what you like to do. I like to describe transactional sales as big-wave surfing: dropping in, going fast, and going hard. The enterprise and long sales-cycle world is more like longboarding, taking your time and just slowly riding the wave.

Dropping in on a wave may be more physically demanding, but the thrill is also more intense because of it. And in transactional sales, we get to experience that thrill more frequently.

Follow the Process

I have surfed the waves of transactional sales. And I have wiped out, but I'm hoping you won't have to—at least not as hard. If you follow the Process and have faith in it, you can be successful.

There are four important steps on this path: build the mindset to succeed, know your stuff, sell it, and stick to the plan.

Build the mindset to succeed. Nothing in sales is more important than how you feel about yourself and what you're doing. You need the right mindset to be open to new ideas, to learn, and to decide that you want to be successful. You control you. Your confidence and your self-esteem are everything. Protect them with great care. Work on them daily. Eliminate anything in your life that does not lift you up.

Know your stuff. You have to know what you're selling and how to sell it. You need to know the product, know why it's important, and know something about your customers and the challenges they face. Then you need to know what you're supposed to say and exactly how to respond in any situation. This makes you a sharper salesperson because you're not thinking of your next line. You are able to listen and pay attention to the more subtle aspects of the interaction. If you are not worried about what you need to say next, you can focus on the needs and problems of the prospect.

Sell it. Sell it, and sell it the right way. The Process is a way to sell based on value. Somebody has a problem, it's important to solve this problem right away, and you're selling the solution. Following the Process leads to small wins, which then lead you to big results. Find pain. Build value. Talk about what the product does. In that order. Do not try to sell it in any other order. Your results will suffer.

Stick to the plan. Life happens. Things change. The only difference between successful people and less successful people is how they handle those changes. The older I get, the more I realize all of our lives are f***ed. Nobody is immune. It's the way we deal with our issues that sets us apart. When you have a problem, don't tweak the steps or focus on the results. Go back to the basics and follow the Process. That's your plan for success.

Now you've been introduced to the Process. And the same Process that you will use to guide the sale is the one you are personally going to use while learning transactional sales. After all, you want to change your life, don't you?

You have a problem, whether it's debt, or an unfulfilling job, or not knowing how to get where you want to go. You should care about that problem: this is your life, and you get only one. You deserve to make it a success. And the solution is in your hands. This book gives you the opportunity to follow the Process from small wins to big rewards.

This Process encompasses both you as the salesperson and what you do when you're selling. I'm going to break both of those down for you throughout the rest of this book, starting with your mindset.

Chapter 2 will give you the mindset you need to succeed.

Build the Mindset
to Succeed

A Reason to Succeed

Everybody has a reason for wanting to succeed. To
say it's about the money is a cop-out. The money is a
means to an end. What will you do with the money?
That's something specific—and that's your reason.

Recently, a young salesperson who works for me
tried to tell me he didn't have a reason for wanting
success. I just looked at him sideways and said, "Come
on, man. I don't believe you." I started asking him
questions about his life, and he revealed that he takes
Uber to work because he doesn't have a car. I pointed
out that might be a reason to work hard and make
a larger commission check next month than the one
he'd just made.

He told me, "I never looked at it that way." From there, I told him to get more specific.

Rather than just having him tell me he wanted a new car, I gave him an assignment. I said, "Go home tonight, go online, and figure out which car you want. What color is it, which dealership has it, and how much does it cost? And I want you to tell me how much money you have now versus how much this car is going to cost. When you do that, tell me how much you need to make in commissions every month to save up for this car."

He came back the next day and said, "Holy crap! If I hit the next commission tier instead of this one, I'm only three or four months away from buying my new car." Lightbulb moment!

On the surface, he didn't think he had goals. But everybody has a reason to succeed if they can just visualize it and get specific about the details.

Win or Lose

That salesperson of mine found his reason to succeed. After that, he needed to find the right mindset.

When you are in the frame of mind to do whatever it takes to win, you have the mindset to succeed. No matter what obstacles are in the way of achieving your goal, you will find a way to get around them. You will rearrange your life to surmount any challenges and accomplish what you set out to do. And once you've done that, you will make more changes to hit your next goal.

If we just dive into transactional sales without the right mindset, we are more likely to quit. We may doubt the product, our company, our boss, and even ourselves. Then we start to give less effort and perform with less passion. We disassociate ourselves so it doesn't hurt if we fail. We are slowly quitting, sometimes even before we realize what we're doing.

My father-in-law once told me, "You can't have one foot on the boat and one foot on the dock. That's going to end badly." And it's the same in transactional sales. You've got to go all in.

To go all in, you first have to figure out why you want to make it happen. Then you can work to develop the right mindset.

Why Make It Happen?

To be successful, you have to want to make it happen more than anything else in the whole world.

Like I said before, transactional sales is often something that people fall into. But no matter where you came from, how do you get yourself to that place where you can make this job a driving force in your life?

When I say, "Make it happen," you first have to know what "it" is. Is it closing a deal? Is it making six figures? Is it becoming a VP or one day starting your own business? Why do you want to change your financial situation? Why do you want to change careers? Why do you want to change your life?

My reason is freedom—the freedom to do what I want when I want. Your reason has to be just as powerful.

Your "why" should start to consume your thoughts. If you just throw it out there without much thought, or without a plan to get there, the sentiment is hollow. But when your why is meaningful to you, you will fall back on it when things start to get tough and you start to struggle. It won't abandon you, even when you might want to abandon yourself. You should spend some time thinking about what motivates you—and why you really want to do well.

The why is going to be different for everyone. And it doesn't matter what your reason is. It just matters that you have one at all times. Once you achieve one of your milestones, it's time to pick another why that is equally powerful.

Once you know what your big goals are, keep them in front of you. I've often read that people who write down their goals and look at them every single day are more likely to achieve them. I know people who tape goals to the dashboards of their cars, or put them underneath their desktop keyboards, or even use one of their goals as their cell phone alarm message. When my alarm goes off, the note says, "No margin for error."

Do goal-setting exercises at the beginning of the year, and do them someplace where you can be alone with your thoughts and away from your normal routine. Then do a reassessment halfway through the year. Ask yourself, "How am I doing so far? What have I crushed? What have I put off? Why did I miss a goal?"

Cross off your goals as you achieve them throughout the year. That satisfaction reminds you why you are doing this. I love crossing things off my to-do list—even if it's a list of groceries! It feels like a small win, and it gives me the positive reinforcement I need to keep striving.

The Mindset to Succeed

You don't want to wait for the right mindset to come to you. You need to seek it out. Success doesn't give you the right mindset; you work on your mindset, and that brings you the success.

The more you can get to a place where you believe in yourself, the product, and the mission, the more it will help your mindset and your confidence. Successful salespeople need to develop and continue to work on the specific traits that help them believe in themselves.

There are seven critical characteristics of a successful sales mindset: confidence, motivation, tenacity, self-improvement, work ethic, ambition, and courage. When you build each of these parts of your mindset, you set yourself up to do whatever it takes to reach your goals.

Confidence. To build your confidence, put it into practical use in your everyday life. Push back on things you don't want, and ask for what you do want.

When I used to fly less frequently, I started making it a point to walk through the priority boarding line at the security checkpoint. I thought if I just acted as though I belonged and was confident enough, I could get through. As far as I can recall, I only got stopped twice.

Do something outside your comfort zone that makes you feel good about yourself. Exercise more, if that gives you confidence. Some people get confidence from knowledge, so learn everything there is to know about a topic. The more positive results you get, the more likely you are to keep doing it, because you feel good about how it's working.

Motivation. How do you keep yourself in the mind-set to succeed once you find it? A lot of it comes from internal motivation, and you need to foster that. But you want to surround yourself with external factors that are going to help you as well.

Examine the people you spend time with. Do they increase your motivation or drag you down? You become who you hang out with, so be aware of their influence on your motivation. Seek out a network of friends and family who understand and support your motivation to succeed and who encourage rather than resent you for it.

I have a group of friends who create a safe place to talk about successes and failures—and to trash-talk each other if one of us has lost some motivation. I would be far less motivated without these essential friendships in my life.

Tenacity. In the transactional sales world, tenacity means not letting temporary defeat get the best of you. You have to be assertive and sometimes aggressive. People may question you, or they may tell you no. By answering their questions or being bold enough to ask for what you want, you build tenacity. You become tough enough to get past any gatekeeper and make it to the right decision maker. You're confident enough to hold firm to the price and bold enough to ask for a shortened time frame for a decision.

After being cooped up in a hospital for so long, I realized that if I needed something, I had to ask for it—and not stop trying until I solved my problem. Learn how to advocate for yourself and be your own best friend. That is tenacity in action.

Self-improvement. You improve yourself through ongoing learning. Just like you want to pay attention to which people you spend your time with; you also want to look at how you spend your time.

Read more. Read about subjects that challenge

your thinking—sales, startups, business, motivation, winners—anything that you think will help you be more productive and successful. When choosing between pumping knowledge into your brain or bleeding it dry watching horrible reality-TV reruns, the choice should be obvious if you really want to succeed.

Talk to people who have done what you want to do. Surround yourself with people who are smarter than you are or who teach you something. Ask for help when you need it. And always look for new ideas so you never end up settling for the status quo.

Work ethic. In order to get to a place you've never been before, you have to be willing to do things you've never done before. Don't keep doing the things that don't work for you.

To hit bigger goals than ever before, you'll have to build up your stamina to work harder and longer than ever before. You'll need to drop the belief systems and the negative labels you've given yourself, like "That's just how I am" or "I'm so ADD." Bullsh*t. That might be something you've struggled with before, or even for most of your life, but it absolutely does not mean that

that is who you are and who you will be forever. Put in the work others are unwilling to do.

I was always a night owl, but I realized that was no longer going to work for me because I sold to the East Coast and lived on the West Coast. I adjusted my hours to maximize my productive work time. I still try to make it a point to be the first one in the office in the morning so I miss the traffic, can work quietly, and set a good example.

Ambition. A lot of people get into sales to make money and rise through the ranks. You have to be ambitious to get into this field. You have to want to make more money. And you have to want the recognition as well as the compensation.

Always want a little bit more, because that will push you to do more. I once heard somebody say that the best salespeople are always in a bit of debt or have overspent their budgets. While I don't recommend that, I can understand the logic behind it. It's just another little something to spur us on to earn more.

I remember wanting to earn five thousand dollars in one month for the first time. After I did that, my next goal was ten thousand. And I just keep increasing it every time I surpass a goal.

Courage. You've got to be brave to sell. You have to have—or develop—thick skin. You are going to fail *way* more often than you'll succeed in this field. You need the courage to believe in yourself and your abilities, even when positive reinforcement appears to be absent. The risks are higher because the upside can be much, much bigger. There is a reason sales is one of the highest-paying professions out there: we are willing to do things most people aren't! And it isn't easy.

The way I see it, I have already faced the hardest thing I will ever face in my life, so why be afraid? I try to keep pushing myself forward even if something is a bit scary.

From Rock Bottom

Sometimes doing whatever it takes to reach your goals means being willing to do a 180 degree with your life.

In 2008, I gave a job interview to a guy I'll call John. At the time, he was in his mid-thirties and had already hit his rock bottom. He'd had a substance abuse problem, and he'd been locked up in jail for almost a year. He had just gone through hell and was trying to come back with his first job after incarceration.

John was ready to change his life. He wanted a new path and a new way forward. But at first, he was just happy to have a job and the chance to earn decent money. I could see he wanted something more for himself, but he didn't quite know how to get there. He was ready to sell, but he had to start with his mindset.

When we first hired him, he thought it would be just another job. Then he found himself in an environment with other people who'd had some difficult challenges, but who also wanted to do something bigger and better with their lives. We pushed him not to accept what life had given him before. And he pushed himself to work on specific changes in the way he thought and viewed the world and in the decisions he made.

I've worked with John at three different companies now, and he's become a good friend of mine. I've watched him transform from a raw and undisciplined mess of an entry-level sales rep to one of the top sales representatives in a company, becoming sales manager, then senior sales manager, and then director of sales. He has grown into an extremely valuable and successful sales leader. He understands people and their motivations, and he uses his personal story to his advantage. He is a huge inspiration in the sales office because he believes in himself and has confidence in his ability to sell.

His story just goes to show that if you get your mindset right, and you're willing to make certain sacrifices and changes, you can turn your life around to become a huge success. Anybody can do it—no matter the obstacles they have to overcome—if they want it enough.

Once you have the mindset to succeed, you are on the path to success. But before you can make a sale, you have to know what you're selling and what to say. The next chapter teaches you to know your stuff.

Chapter 3

Know Your Stuff

My Own Little World

All salespeople have had moments where they've been caught not knowing their stuff. Hell, part of why we ended up in sales is because we know how to wing it and to freestyle our way out of trouble and into a position of strength. Our charm and charisma get us where we need to be.

In my first-ever sales job, I was selling online lead-generation tools for real estate agents. We had tall cubicles, so I couldn't see anybody around me. I was in my own little world. It was extremely isolating. I either knew what to do or I didn't; those were my only options. I was not going to receive any support.

When I had been working there a couple of weeks,

I was on the phone with a prospect who asked me a question I didn't know how to answer. I didn't know my stuff, and I panicked. It was so important to me to make that sale, and I could see it slipping away before my eyes.

I put the phone on mute and wedged it against my shoulder. Then I leaned my chair way back and craned my neck, frantically trying to make eye contact with someone in any direction who could give me the answer.

The person on the phone was still talking, and I wasn't listening at all. By the time my neighbor told me what to say and I unmuted the phone, I was chiming in with the answer to a question that was two minutes old. I had completely ignored everything that had been said in the meantime.

In the end, I didn't make the sale. But I learned my lesson. There's nothing wrong with not having an answer one time. The real stupidity would be doing nothing about it. So I thought of every possible scenario that might trip me up. I wrote up the best possible response for each. Then I set out to memorize the list . . . right after I crossed off that day's question.

I wasn't going to make that mistake again.

Know Your Stuff

When I couldn't answer the question I was asked, it was completely my fault. I could've blamed it on a lack of training or a lack of coaching from my manager, but at the end of the day, I didn't know my stuff.

Knowing your stuff means that you know what you're selling and how it needs to be sold, and you know what you're talking about. That may seem really obvious, but the better you understand the product you're trying to sell, the better you'll be able to handle questions and objections. And if you combine your charm and wittiness with knowing what to say, rather than winging it, you're going to close more deals. So why do so many salespeople settle for only the most basic grasp of their product?

When you cut corners or try to fake it, trusting your talent over training, you don't learn the material very well, and it messes up the rest of the Process. In essence, you are teaching yourself bad habits that will not benefit you in the long run. Someone is going to find out. You may be able to get away with it a few times, but people are going to realize that you are bullsh*tting them.

On the other hand, when you are well prepared,

you can have fun and move faster toward your goals. You can pay closer attention to what the prospect is saying and feeling. You can anticipate where the call is headed next. So why not know everything important?

There are two aspects to knowing your stuff. First, you have to know your product. Then you have to know your script.

Know Your Product

You don't have to love your product, but it does help. You will be more motivated to understand it and all its benefits for your customers. But whether you love it or not, you have to develop a thorough understanding of the product before you can sell it. You can't sell it if you don't know what it is.

To know your product, you need to know how it works, what pain points it solves, and what value it provides. You also want to know why this particular product or solution is a "must have" instead of a "nice to have." Why is this an urgent purchase for the customer? Take the time to learn everything the product offers that will matter to your customer.

If you have multiple products, educate yourself on

all of them as much as you can. Otherwise, you miss out on opportunities because you don't know how to speak to the whole suite of products. If you sell only one product in the suite because you don't know the rest, you may only be able to sell to one type of prospect. That's like fishing with a small hook instead of a big net. When you expand your knowledge, you naturally expand your success.

There are several things you can do to really know your product. First, read the manual, pay attention during the training, and take notes. Ask the product people how it works on the back end. Use the product if you are able. Play around with it as if you were the customer. Know how to navigate it, and spend time finding its best aspects—the things you can feel passionate and fired up to talk about. Spend time talking with people who use the product. Completely familiarize yourself with it, and keep up to date with new packages or details.

A word of caution: knowing everything about the product does *not* mean you have to cover everything about it with prospects. It is possible to overwhelm them with information, which slows down the sales cycle and can ultimately result in overselling your way out of a deal.

That's why you need to learn the right way to talk about the product and know your script.

Know Your Script

You know your product. Now you need to know what to say about it—and how and when to say it. Trying to just wing it and see what happens is not a good idea. It's better to have a game plan you can execute and refer back to as needed.

Depending on your employer or career stage, you will either write your own script or take what somebody else has done and master it—only then trying to improve on it.

To build your script from scratch, you need to start pitching. Pitch to yourself, the mirror, your significant other, and anyone else willing to let you practice. Start with a "perfect" pitch, one where a prospect doesn't push back at all and things go perfectly all the way to a close. This will become the basis for your visualization of how calls should go.

As you try to sell the product, play around with what works. When something feels as if it's starting to work and you're making some progress, write it down. I like to type out a whole simulated conversation.

Test it, listen to your pitch, and improve on it until it works in a practice environment. Then test it on real prospects.

When you're given a script that is already written, don't try to reinvent the wheel—especially if you are a new salesperson just getting into the industry. The people at your company have had some success with that script, and you need to follow that success. Think about it: why would they give you something if they didn't think it was the best possible way for you to succeed?

Either way, your script should be a living, breathing document. It shouldn't stay stagnant. The pitch that works today will be different from the one that worked three years ago. When you first learn about a topic, it may take you a long time to explain it. But as you develop your pitch over months and years, you'll get better at breaking it down to its simplest elements. Then you can take a look at it every six months or so and ask, "Is this still relevant? Does it still work? Can I make it shorter or easier?"

The final piece is just studying your script any way you can. You can't overdo it. Read it over breakfast, recite it in your car, and practice while you wait in line at the coffee shop. The routine matters much more than the words. The repetition is critical to your initial growth and success. Treat it like you're studying for a college exam. Memorize it completely. The more you do it, the more easily it will flow out of you. Without realizing it, you'll be able to put your own personality into the script and make it your own. Know it so well that you would be able to pick up right in the middle if you heard somebody else pitching it!

In fact, one trick to determine whether you know the script well enough is to try doing a relay race with a group of people. See if you can pick up the script right where the person before you leaves off. It's pretty cool when a group of salespeople can finish each other's sentences!

The Flip Side of the Coin

At the beginning of this chapter, I told you the story about a time when I didn't know what I was supposed to say. That was really chaotic, stressful, and ridiculous.

The flip side of that coin is knowing your stuff. When you do, you are so confident in what you're selling that you can ask the prospect a ton of questions.

You are able to sit back and listen to the answers, which allows you to guide the conversation.

Eventually, I got to that place with that first product and script. I wasn't rushed, worried, or nervous about what to say. Instead, I was patient, and I waited for my moment. Then the prospect said the words I was waiting to hear: "Tell me about what you guys do. I want to know. I'm interested." Those words gave me permission to talk about our solution. I got the green light to proceed toward a close.

Those are the kinds of sales experiences you're looking for. When you know your stuff, you're always prepared to find those experiences.

Now you know your product and what to say. So what comes next? It's time to sell it.

Chapter 4

Sell It

Connection to Addiction

As I told you in the introduction, I have based my sales Process on the addiction model. But no one taught me that concept.

In 2010, I was the Vice President of Sales at Main Street Hub. I'd had about six years of sales leadership experience at that time. I went to our office in New York City to give a talk to twenty-five salespeople about sales and performance. I had taught and explained things the same way a million times before.

This time would be different.

"I don't get why sales have to flow in a certain way," a young guy in his early twenties said that day. I looked at him for a second. I had to come up with an analogy that would make sense of it all. And the connection to the addiction model just came out. It was raw and personal and, in my opinion, a perfect description.

Maybe it came from having been sick and in the hospital on pain medication for four years. From a physical standpoint, I knew some of what being an addict was like. I also have friends who have struggled with substance abuse their whole lives. So it might have come from that place of familiarity; it was something I could understand. And sometimes you have to describe things in a gritty way to connect with your audience.

Whatever the reason, it worked. I could see from the nodding heads and fixed eyes that I had hit on something. After the talk, one of the sales leaders in the office came up to me and said, "That's a really good way to explain that." I started using it more and more. I refined the Process and the language around it. By the time I got to my next company, it just became part of the lingo. "Sales is like addiction . . ."

That day, my sales Process got a name.

Follow the Steps

The Process is really easy to remember because it is so simple. There are only four main steps at the core of the addiction model and, therefore, at the heart of my sales Process.

First, you get prospects to admit they have a problem. Then you make them understand why they should care that they have this problem, and you make them want to solve it immediately. Then and only then are they going to be open to hearing about solutions to that particular problem, and you can talk about what you do.

Pain. Value. Urgency. Solution. This is the way you close transactional sales with confidence and consistency.

You cannot use the steps of the Process out of order. If you do, you won't be very successful. You may be in the right frame of mind and be prepared, but you will have no idea how to execute the sale. If you screw up the sequencing, the message just does not have the same impact. If you follow every step in this particular way, though, it will give you the best chance for success.

In transactional sales, you are typically considered

a solid contributor if you are able to close a deal every two days. The best of the best can get around one deal a day. You are an absolute rock star if you close the deal on one out of every one hundred cold calls.

The model I am showing you will work for every product I've ever seen in the transactional sales world. I have taught folks from companies all across America and in Europe about this Process, and I have seen them implement it with great success.

You simply have to trust it, practice it, perfect it, and stick with it.

The Process

The Process should go the same way every time. Pay attention to it because, if done consistently, it will work and it will yield you the best results.

The Process has four main steps, but those steps are broken down further to create the ideal call flow. The call flow has nine steps: talk to a decision maker, find the pain, build value, create urgency, talk about what you do, discuss opportunities, attempt to close, deal with objections, and close or set a follow-up.

1. ***Make sure you're talking to a decision maker.*** The first step is to make sure you're talking to the right person. This will be the person who handles everything having to do with the product or service you're offering. Ask, "Am I talking to the owner? Are you the only decision maker?" You don't want to waste your time talking to somebody who's not critical to the decision-making process. The great thing about transactional sales is that you rarely have more than one decision maker and usually very few gatekeepers to get past.

2. ***Find the pain.*** This is where the addiction model really starts to take shape. Once you have the right person on the phone, you have to get this person to admit he or she has a problem. Dig for information about his or her business, background, experience, or comfort level. Ask questions that drive toward the answer you want, which is "I don't know how to do that," or "I've never done that before." Now you've found the pain point. This is the most important

part of the entire Process. It is not good enough to tell prospects they have a problem. They have to admit it themselves!

3. ***Build value.*** Once they've admitted that they have this pain point, it's your job to make them understand why they should care about this problem. Even when people know they have a problem, they may not truly see the value in doing something about it. As you educate them, they should begin to want to make a change. Think about functioning addicts. They might be aware they have a problem but are not yet compelled to do anything about it. They don't see the value in making a change yet. That is your job—to make them understand the value. That rolls into the next step, which is to . . .

4. ***Create urgency.*** Make them understand that their problem is mission critical. It's not a paper cut; it's a severed limb demanding urgent attention. They are losing business every single day by not doing something to fix the problem. The more

specific and personal you can make the story, the better. If you can provide concrete data and dollar amounts, do so. Talk about what their competitors are doing and how their market share is at risk. Paint a picture that compels them to act sooner rather than later.

5. ***Solution.*** Once prospects admit they have a problem, understand why they should care about it, and feel they should do something about it right away, you have permission to talk about what your company does. Then and only then! This is the part every prospect wants you to talk about right away. Don't do it! First, get them so interested that they are nearly begging you to talk about what you do. Now they will pay attention as you explain the product or solution. Keep it simple, and use the script you prepared.

6. ***Discuss opportunities.*** After talking about what you do, it's time to give a little summary. Recap the problem so that prospects

understand why it's important to do something about it and how you can help. Show how your product will benefit them. Summarize it in a really clear-cut way that presents a compelling story. Again, make your analogies or examples as real and specific as possible. Get them to *see* the outcome in their minds.

7. ***Attempt to close.*** If, after following all the other steps, you present that compelling story in the right way, the table is set to go into a trial close. You can say, "There are a couple of different ways we can partner with you." Then walk through those. Ease them into an entry-level price point, so they don't get spooked. Show them a mid-tier option and then a high-end option. No one wants to be the big spender, but people don't want to be the cheapskate either. Give them your recommendation, then ask what makes the most sense to them. Guide them into the close by steering them into the middle option, which is where most people end up.

8. ***Deal with objections and rebut them.***
    Inevitably, when you go to close the deal,
    there will be objections. All the doubts,
    fears, and budget constraints the prospect
    has are going to rear their heads. Be pre-
    pared to deal with these objections and
    provide rebuttals. You've got this! You
    know why? Because you scripted all this
    out, rehearsed it, and are therefore com-
    pletely prepared to answer any objections.
    Walk your prospect through your way
    of thinking, so the person sees that the
    objection is not a big deal; it's something
    to work through. You will be in a loop
    of dealing with objections and rebuttals
    until you finally get some indication that
    the flow is going to conclude in one of
    two desirable ways, described in the next
    step, or in one disappointing way—with
    a no.

9. ***Close or set a follow-up appointment.***
    Once you've dealt with all the objections,
    your job is to try to close once again. If
    the deal's not going to close, then close

on the next best thing: a follow-up. Set a specific day and time to talk again, so the prospect has some time to think about it. Lock down the appointment with a calendar invitation. Invite the prospect to do research and come prepared with any further questions. Then politely ask, "Next time we talk, all I ask is that we can arrive at a yes or no decision. Does that sound fair to you?" And that's the best you can do. That's still a win.

The Emergency Room

When I train salespeople, I tell them to think of the Process as though they're trying to get someone with a cut to go to the hospital.

First, you notice the cut on the person. Then you get the person to notice it too. You make this individual understand that he or she needs to address the injury. It's the best thing to do, health-wise.

You can create urgency by expanding that awareness, saying, for example, "Actually, this cut is more serious than you think it is." At that point, the person will notice how much the cut is bleeding. You don't want to freak him or her out, but you point out that the cut may have hit an artery.

Finally the person says, "I need to do something about it now!"

That is the time to say that you are taking the person to the hospital. You can discuss the benefits of stitches versus butterfly bandages on the way. Maybe the person is afraid of needles or objects, saying, "I don't have insurance!" No matter what, you have to get him or her to the emergency room.

So you close the deal. You discuss the concerns, but you take action and help save the person. If you need to, you also schedule a follow-up appointment with the doctor.

But if you do these steps out of order—rushing people to the ER before they know how badly they're hurt—you're going to meet with a lot of resistance. For the greatest success, always follow the Process of the addiction model, and do it in the correct order.

Now you know every step you need to take to close the deal. You may be tempted to make some changes, but why would you? The next chapter is all about sticking to the plan.

Chapter 5

Stick to the Plan

Off a Cliff

In the world of transactional sales, messing with success can lead to a horrible downward spiral.

When I was at OutboundEngine, we sold e-mail and social media marketing services to local small-business owners. A relatively new team member (I'll call him Bob) came in, and he had never done anything like this job before. He was a born hustler from the streets of NYC, so I knew he could be good. He did what he was taught when he first got there. He worked really hard right out of the gate, implemented feedback well, asked for help, and began crushing it.

Then suddenly and without reason, he just fell off a (figurative) cliff.

Because he had been doing so well, he had been rewarded with inbound leads, which was pretty rare. And while he had been following the Process for cold calls, he started doing things differently with inbound leads.

Although he had been told to "stick with what works," Bob started to cut corners. He didn't spend as much time educating prospects. His results started to suffer, and he couldn't understand why. He was struggling, and he got stuck in his own head. He doubted the product, doubted his abilities, and even started making excuses, saying he doubted the leads were any good. By the next quarter, he had gone from hitting 300 percent of his quota down to just 20 percent.

Fortunately, Bob had an "aha!" moment after about a month and a half of struggling. He realized where he'd gone wrong. It had happened when he had stopped sticking to the plan and started thinking he could do it in a simpler, easier way, despite having zero prior experience.

So he rededicated himself to following the Process—in the correct order. He knew that it had worked for him before and would continue to do so. And he saw it again: his results went back up. In fact, after a year and a half at that company, he became one of its highest producers.

Bob learned his lesson about going off-Process, and his turnaround has led to his continued success. Not everybody can make it back to the top of the mountain after falling down, and it's certainly easier if you can follow the same process and roads that got you there the first time.

A Repeatable Process

Bob knew his plan. He just had to learn to stick to it. He had to learn to trust it.

When you want to create a repeatable process, you make a strategic plan, and you stick to that plan. Once that process is working, you don't deviate from it. You continue with it and play the odds for success. It becomes math.

What did my Process look like? I arrived at work at six in the morning and started calling the East Coast. I made twenty calls before I did anything else each day—no bathroom break, no water break, no snack break, no checking e-mail or fantasy football until those calls were made. I avoided discussions at the office with others who were complaining. I knew I needed a certain number of appointments scheduled each day in order to avoid peaks and valleys, and I did not leave until I hit that target.

I would leave in the afternoon and head to the beach to surf until it got dark, letting the cold Pacific Ocean wash away the stress of a hard day of selling. When I got home, I opened my laptop and sent out prospecting e-mails—lots of e-mails—before I went to bed. That was my daily grind back then. That Process positioned me for success. If you trust in it, the math will play out in your favor.

If you make a certain number of dials, you will get through to a certain number of decision makers, which will turn into a certain number of deals. That plan will work. If you don't stick to the plan, it is very difficult to know what is working and what is going wrong. You can end up losing confidence and second-guessing yourself. When you stick to the Process, however, the numbers show results in terms of your bottom-line success.

But before you can stick to the plan, you first have to know what to expect.

Manage Your Expectations

The easiest way to stick to the plan is to manage your expectations. And the best way to manage your expectations is to know the numbers.

Sales is full of rejection. Knowing what to expect is the antidote. Knowing your metrics and the math behind how your business works can help you let go of a ton of stress, frustration, and anxiety.

A really successful salesperson might close one out of every one hundred cold calls or one out of every ten appointments. Compared with other industries, that's not a very good success rate. If a basketball player shot 1 percent or even 10 percent, he or she wouldn't be playing for very long. Need a different sports analogy? If a baseball player is called out in seven of ten at bats during the season, he will hit .300 for the year. If you hit .300 a year for long enough, you have a great shot at being a Hall of Famer. Salespeople would *kill* for those numbers!

But in transactional sales, it simply isn't possible. You'd be a superstar if you failed ninety-nine times out of one hundred. That is a f*** ton of rejection for us to deal with, is it not? When you understand these dynamics, you can prepare yourself mentally for the fact that you are going to fail way more often than you're going to succeed.

When your expectations are reasonable, you will find it much easier to stick to the plan.

Stick to the Plan

There are three categories where you really want to stick to the plan: your office culture, your sales training, and your healthy routine.

Office culture. You need to understand what the culture of your sales office is and how it works for you. It should be conducive to making sales.

There are cultural movements going on right now in the startup world, with people trying to weave in lots of work-life balance. For example, some companies allow you to take your pet to work. But in sales, that may not be the kind of culture that gives you the best results. You are trying to eliminate distractions, and people's dogs need exercise, food, water, and attention. All of those things take you away from the calls you need to make. Different jobs need different things.

You need to make sure the office you work for is set

up to give you the greatest success. Is it a sales-oriented culture where salespeople are valued and respected? Does the leadership empower the sales organization and provide as many benefits and rewards to people as possible? Is the right kind of attitude pervasive in the office? You don't want to work in a place where there's a lot of complaining, but rather in an atmosphere of overcoming challenges and celebrating successes.

As a salesperson, the more you align yourself with a culture that sets you up for success, the better results you'll get.

Training. Learn what works best for you and your type of learning process. Then make a plan for training, and stick to it.

You have to know your product and know your script, so come up with a rhythm to aid that learning. Try all different types of learning. See, for example, whether auditory is better than visual for you. I used to listen to Brian Tracy on my commute home every day when I was first getting started in sales. I learned some great techniques just by listening to those CDs over and over. Study the different parts of your product and its features at night. Spend an hour every day— before work, at lunch, or after work—role-playing and rehearsing your pitch. When you make this a routine, you will find the rhythm that allows you to be as successful as possible.

Your organization should also have support pieces in place, including a culture that promotes growth and development. If the company offers training, go. Seek help, and be as proactive as you can. Look at each leader or top performer as a resource for getting as much help as possible. If you don't have an environment that gives you much help, it's even more critical that you find a way to do it on your own. Create a situation for yourself that allows you to do your best.

A healthy routine. You want your habits to create your best self, so you can come to work at 100 percent every day. That means you want to develop a routine outside of work that is healthy and helpful to your success professionally.

You need to get the right amount of sleep. It's very difficult to show up to work at eight o'clock if you've been out partying until three in the morning. You'll be off to a slow start, and that can really hold you back. I try to wake up early, as often as my health allows.

Eat the right foods, and find a way to exercise. Otherwise, your health may be negatively affected, which means you may not be coming into the office as much. And that won't just prevent you from closing deals that day, but will also prevent you from building a pipeline that could provide deals in the future. I know getting exercise for me is unlikely to happen if I don't do it first thing in the morning, and it's a key ingredient to my happiness and health. I like getting it done early when it's quiet and I have no distractions. That is my rhythm. Once you find a rhythm that works for you, you want to do everything you can to stay right in that pocket.

Sales is an extremely stressful and emotionally charged profession. Finding healthy outlets to manage the stress is an essential part of becoming a great salesperson. Try not to get too up or too down emotionally. Surround yourself with people who do not add emotional weight to your life, but who support your efforts and positively influence you.

If you can do these things, you are demonstrating a commitment to success and following the Process.

Stick to the Recipe

One of the things that has made me a successful sales rep is that when I find something that works in any part of my life, I do not change it. Alternatively, I know someone who loves to tinker and experiment and is sometimes frustrated by the results (albeit in a totally different capacity). Sorry, Janet, but it's just a perfect story.

My wife likes to bake. And she's always tinkering with the recipes for pancakes, muffins, and other treats, adding a pinch of something here and a dash of something else there. They always taste good, but they never taste the same from one batch to the next.

Every now and then, she will make one batch of pancakes that is absolutely perfect. Our kids and I tell her, "You nailed it!" And the next time we have pancakes, I think to myself, "She's probably going to make them the same way as last time, because they were perfect." But nope. She tinkered again. And sometimes they are not nearly as good. (Sorry, but it's true.)

Don't sell this way!

You have the right mindset. You know your stuff. And you know the Process. You've made a plan, and you're going to stick to it. You've found success. But how do you know when it's time to push yourself to move forward? In the final chapter, we'll take a look at what's over the next horizon.

Chapter 6

The Next Move

Catapult to Change

Big growth points in my life often come when I listen to that voice that says, "I need something new. I need something more. I need to go bigger!" Sometimes it takes an event to catapult you forward.

For me, one of those events was a surf trip to Central America.

I had known for some time that I needed a change. I had started to become a little frustrated in my role at work. I was interested in what other people were doing but bored with what I was doing. I was getting restless.

I had some vacation time due, so I went on a surfing trip. I found myself in the middle of nowhere, in a small Central American country, with a bunch of my oldest friends. We went all the way to the Pacific Coast, to a place with some of the best waves we could find. We were the only people at this little surf village. We had the beach all to ourselves for an entire week. It was like having our own private surf resort. The exercise and isolation were exactly what I needed to bring about clarity.

I had a lot of time to relax, think, and reflect. I had conversations with my friends and got their feedback and advice. And sometimes when you remove yourself from the hectic everyday stress and chaos of your life, the right idea comes to you. I was somewhere serene, out in nature, and that gave me a sense of clarity.

That trip was the impetus to make a decision I had been afraid to make for a while. It's where I really recognized and acknowledged, "Oh yeah, I'm done." And it was time to move on.

When I got back, I told my employer I was done. We parted ways.

I didn't know what I was going to do next. So for twenty-four hours, it was rough. All the fear and frustration of making a big change came up. *Oh sh*t, what just happened?* I thought. *What am I going to do?* I think it is important to allow yourself to really feel the emotion rather than suppress it. It becomes unhealthy only when you start to dwell on it and can't move on.

When I woke up on day two, I thought, *Okay, now I get to figure out what I'm going to do next. Time to get to work!*

And suddenly life became really exciting. It was almost addicting in a way—that rush of having so many opportunities and getting to decide which one was the right one. It crushed the fear and frustration. And opportunities started flying at me almost faster than I could keep up. I felt secure that this was the best thing that could've happened to me.

I was on my way to something bigger. And I've been repeating that process ever since.

Time to Move On

To keep growing, you have to keep moving. And sometimes that means moving away from something easy and familiar.

You have to recognize when you've hit the ceiling in a certain role or at a particular organization. When you decide to push yourself forward to find the next challenge, you are saying that you won't settle for mediocrity.

You should always try to find a way to one-up yourself. Sometimes that means taking a leap of faith. Faith in yourself is a prerequisite to success.

In the previous chapter, I said that once you find something that works, you should just keep doing it. And that holds true: you keep doing it until the job is done and there is nothing left for you to do, nowhere left for you to grow.

When there is nothing left for you there, it's time to move on.

Once you've outgrown a particular role, go find the next thing. The right thing. Then challenge yourself with that new thing, and figure out how to excel at it. Do all the right things consistently to remain excellent, until you hit a different ceiling. You will keep hitting them if you keep crushing it, because it never stops. And neither should you.

You never stop growing. You never stop learning and improving and trying to be better. And you should never stop pushing toward a successful, fulfilling life. I am hoping a successful career in sales is a part of that!

The Next Step of the Journey

At the end of the day, we are all on a journey. It's a journey of self-discovery and self-fulfillment. But you don't have to travel in silence, alone on that path.

I encourage you to find a mentor, coach, or boss who has figured it out, and then attach yourself at the hip to that person. Get a direct line into the advice and insight he or she has to offer. I didn't have much of that, especially at the beginning of my journey, and it would have been a lot easier for me if I had.

Gone are the days when people go to work for one company for the next forty years of their lives and just work their way up slowly. People don't do that anymore. Younger generations don't think that way. What you want are big paydays and fancy jobs, and you want them yesterday.

So it's on me to provide you with the type of training and skills you need to achieve the success required to move up. I want to help everybody get to the next level and keep going.

I would love to help you get on the path to where you want to go. You can connect with me easily on LinkedIn and Twitter, and I am happy to be a resource or recommend resources from my years in sales all over the country and different parts of the world. You can also find me at my website: <u>www.scottleeseconsulting.com</u>.

I urge you to use everything available to you, and do whatever you have to do, to keep moving forward on the path to success. There is absolutely no reason you cannot succeed.

Find Success

I hope you feel fired up to kick-start your sales journey using the Process I have detailed in this book—especially if you're on a path similar to the one I've traveled.

Remember, I started as an entry-level inside salesperson who had zero experience and zero background in business. And I tapped into something I didn't know was there. Once I found it, I achieved success that went beyond anything I could have ever imagined. And if I can do it, so can you.

Let this knowledge light a fire inside of you. You've always known it was there. Now it's time to let it burn bright enough to impel you to make some changes, push yourself, and take some chances.

I want you to succeed in sales. But more than

that, I want you to find success in life. You control you, and the only thing that determines your success is how much you want to make it happen.

Stay addicted to the Process, and watch your life take off.

ABOUT THE AUTHOR

Scott Leese is one of the top startup sales leaders in the country. He has built and scaled thriving sales teams at numerous multimillion-dollar companies and advised on many more. Leese's near-death experience with illness led him to discover sales and startups, where he achieved success using the dedication, process, and drive to compete that he had honed as a multisport athlete and through the fight to take back his health.

Named one of the Top 25 Most Influential Inside Sales Professionals by AA-ISP, Leese is the Founder of Scott Leese Consulting, LLC and serves as the Senior Vice President of Sales at Qualia Labs, Inc. He has built and advised successful sales teams across the globe, including Austin, San Diego, Portland, and Berlin, Germany, Phoenix, New York City, and Los Angeles, and all over the San Francisco Bay Area.

An avid traveler and rabid sports fan, Leese tries to live life like every day is game day. He enjoys coaching, surfing, and savoring the finest tequila. Leese lives in Austin, Texas, with his wife, Janet; their two boys, Brayden and Caleb; and the family dog, Loki.

Ready to take your sales game to the next level? Scott Leese Consulting has the tools to help you burn through your obstacles and nail the success you've been hungry for. Scott offers:

- Top-to-bottom value analysis that reveals why people buy
- A proven sales process that works for any product or service
- Career development to help you hit your real goals
- Training that lights a fire under you and your sales team
- KPI tracking that drives your success with measurable progress
- Sales tools to sharpen your competitive advantage
- Compensation plans that attract and keep great talent

For more information, visit <u>www.scottleesecon-</u><u>sulting.com</u>.

You can connect with Scott on

- Twitter: <u>twitter.com/sleese555</u>
- LinkedIn: <u>www.linkedin.com/in/scottleese</u>

Made in the USA
San Bernardino, CA
30 October 2017